Creature Features

Anita Ganeri • Illustrated by Steve Fricker

Heinemann

HOW IT WORKS – CREATURE FEATURES was produced by Marshall Editions, 170 Piccadilly, London, W1V 9DD.

Editor: Claire Berridge
Designers: Ian Winton, Steve Prosser
Managing Editor: Kate Phelps
Design Manager: Ralph Pitchford
Art Director: Branka Surla
Editorial Director: Cynthia O'Brien
Production: Janice Storr, Selby Sinton
Jacket Designer: Sandra Begnor
Researcher: Lynda Wargen

First published in Great Britain in 1997 by Heinemann Children's Reference, an imprint of Heinemann Educational Publishers, Halley Court, Jordan Hill, Oxford OX2 8EJ, a division of Reed Educational and Professional Publishing Limited.

MADRID ATHENS
FLORENCE PRAGUE WARSAW
PORTSMOUTH NH CHICAGO SAO PAULO MEXICO
SINGAPORE TOKYO MELBOURNE AUCKLAND
IBADAN GABORONE JOHANNESBURG KAMPALA NAIROBI

ISBN 0-431-06990-5

British Library Cataloguing-In-Publication Data.
A catalogue record for this book is available from the British Library.

Printed and bound in Italy by Officine Grafiche de Agostini, Novara.
Originated in Singapore by Master Image.

CONTENTS

ALL ABOUT ANIMALS

Animals are truly amazing! There are millions and millions of different kinds. They are divided into groups depending on how their beastly bits fit together. Animals with bones inside their bodies are called vertebrates (fish, amphibians, mammals, reptiles and birds). Those without bones are known as invertebrates (crustaceans, arachnids, insects and molluscs). Both of these big groups are divided into the smaller ones pictured here.

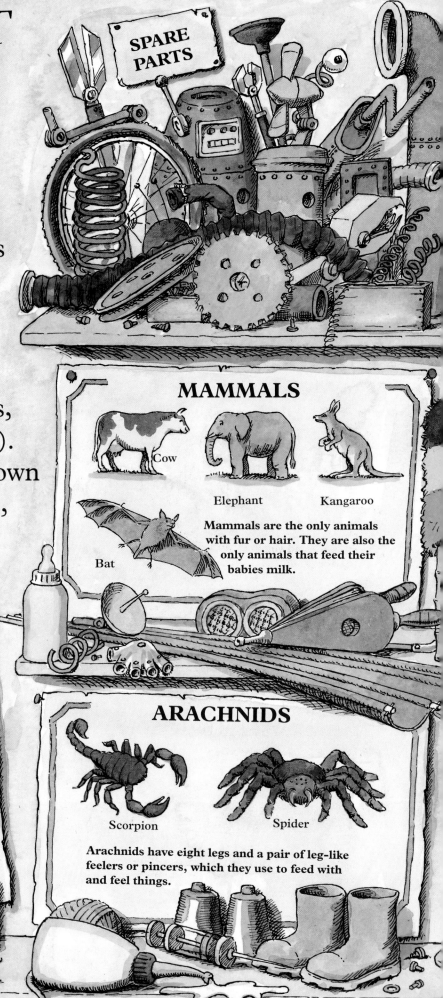

SPARE PARTS

MAMMALS

Cow

Elephant

Kangaroo

Bat

Mammals are the only animals with fur or hair. They are also the only animals that feed their babies milk.

CRUSTACEANS

Lobster

Prawn

Crab

Crustaceans have hard, tough cases around their soft bodies. Most crustaceans live in water, but wood lice live on land.

ARACHNIDS

Scorpion

Spider

Arachnids have eight legs and a pair of leg-like feelers or pincers, which they use to feed with and feel things.

FISH

Shark

Eel

Salmon

Fish live in the salty sea and in freshwater. They have fins for swimming and gills (instead of lungs) for breathing.

AMPHIBIANS

Frog

Giant salamander

Toad

Amphibians can live in water and on land, but they always go back into the water to lay their eggs.

REPTILES

Snake

Tortoise

Reptiles have scaly skin and lay their eggs on land. Did you know that dinosaurs were reptiles, too?

BIRDS

Chicken

Hummingbird

The beastly bits of birds include feathers, wings and beaks. Birds are the only animals in the world with feathers.

INSECTS

Ant

Fly

Stag beetle

Insects have six jointed legs. There are more types of insect than any other group of animals in the world.

MOLLUSCS

Octopus

Clam

Snail

Most molluscs have hard shells to protect their soft, squishy bodies. Some molluscs live on land; others dwell in the sea.

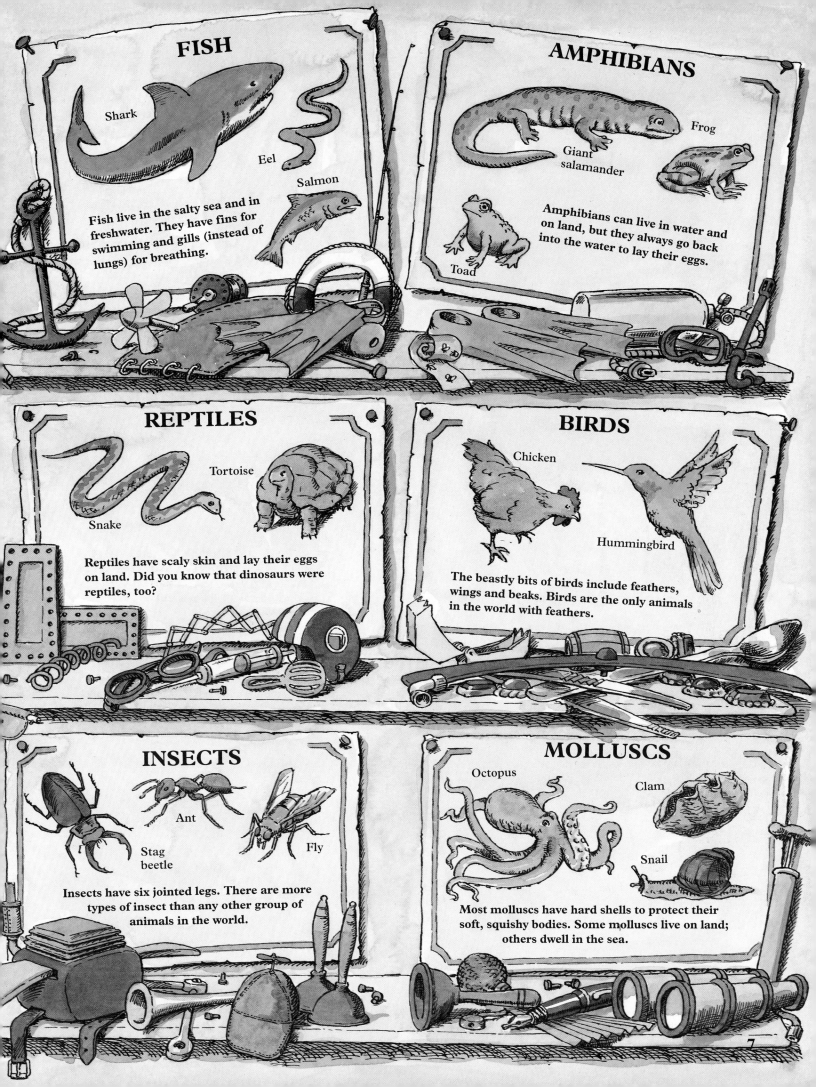

7

ALL ABOUT COWS

Next time you take a cool, refreshing sip of milk, spare a thought for the cow it came from. Each year cows give us millions of gallons of milk to drink or to make into yoghurt and cheese. Now, to all the bits of cows!

Cows have very long eyelashes for brushing away pesky flies.

Furry ears keep out unwanted insects.

Cows have strong teeth for grinding up their food of grass and plants.

Spike
(Horn)

Feather duster
(Eyelashes)

Keep Out

Fly Screen
(Ear)

Grinder
(Mouth and teeth)

Food Processor
(Stomach)

1

2

HOW MUCH MILK?
A cow makes about two and a half gallons of milk a day. Over a year, this is enough to fill up 20 bathtubs.

Shoe
(Hoof)

The cow's hooves are like huge shoes that protect its feet.

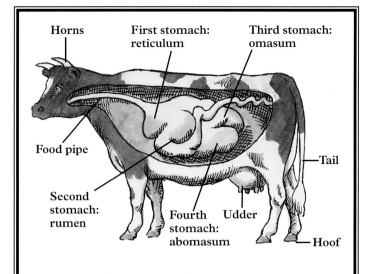

A cow has four stomachs. When a cow eats grass, it grinds it up in its mouth and the goodness the grass contains is taken out. The first stomach makes the grass into little balls. These go back into the cow's mouth to be chewed again.

Horns · **First stomach: reticulum** · **Third stomach: omasum**

Food pipe · **Tail**

Second stomach: rumen · **Fourth stomach: abomasum** · **Udder** · **Hoof**

WHAT IS A COW?

Cows belong to the group of animals called mammals. They all make milk to feed their babies. Milk contains water and lots of nourishment, everything a baby needs to grow up big and strong.

The chewed grass passes through the other stomachs, and water and the good things in it are taken out and used to make milk.

The milk squirts out through udders on the cow's stomach. The udders are similar to the teats on a baby's bottle.

The cow's long, hairy tail makes a perfect flyswatter as it swishes from side to side.

Flyswat (Tail)

Cowpat

Baby's bottle (Udder)

Any waste from food digestion is pushed out to make a cowpat. *Splat!*

How do you like your eggs? Boiled? Fried? Millions of eggs are eaten each year. Most of these come from chickens. A chicken can lay an egg a day. If the egg is fertilized it will produce a chick. We eat the unfertilized eggs. Now let's see how the chicken produces these eggs.

When a chick is ready to hatch, a tiny tapping noise comes from its shell. The chick has a knobby bump on its beak. It uses this like a pick to chip away at the shell. Then it struggles out.

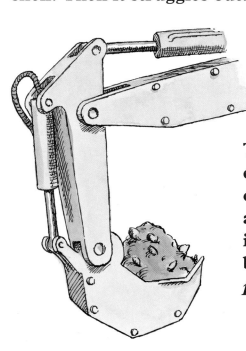

Tweezers (Beak)

The raw materials for making an egg come from the corn, seeds and worms the chicken eats.

The chicken can pick up corn, insects and worms with its short, sharp beak – *peck! peck! peck!*

Mechanical digger (Claw)

Chickens have digger-like claws for uncovering grains of corn, seeds, and . . . worms!

On its journey through the chicken, different parts are added to the egg. First comes the yolk, then the egg white and finally the shell.

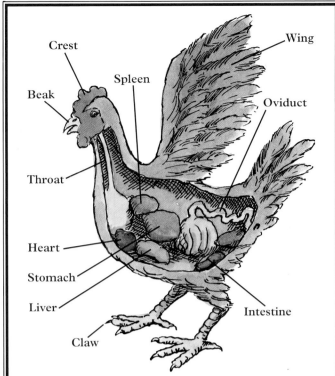

Crest
Wing
Spleen
Beak
Oviduct
Throat
Heart
Stomach
Liver
Intestine
Claw

WHAT IS A CHICKEN?
A chicken is a type of bird. You can tell this by its feathers, wings, and beak. All birds lay hard-shelled eggs, which they keep warm and safe until they hatch.

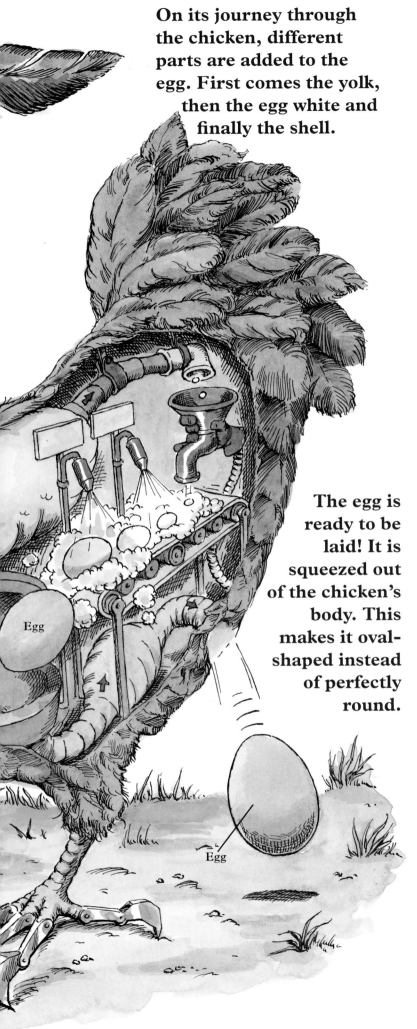

The egg is ready to be laid! It is squeezed out of the chicken's body. This makes it oval-shaped instead of perfectly round.

Egg

Egg

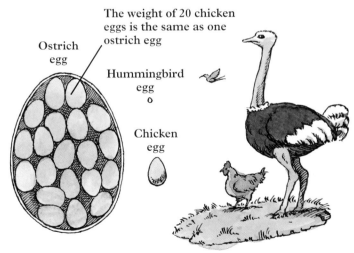

The weight of 20 chicken eggs is the same as one ostrich egg

Ostrich egg

Hummingbird egg

Chicken egg

RECORD BREAKERS!
The world's biggest bird lays the world's biggest eggs. A single ostrich egg weighs as much as 20 chicken eggs. Its shell is so strong that you can stand on it. The smallest and most delicate eggs are laid by tiny hummingbirds. They are barely as big as baked beans.

11

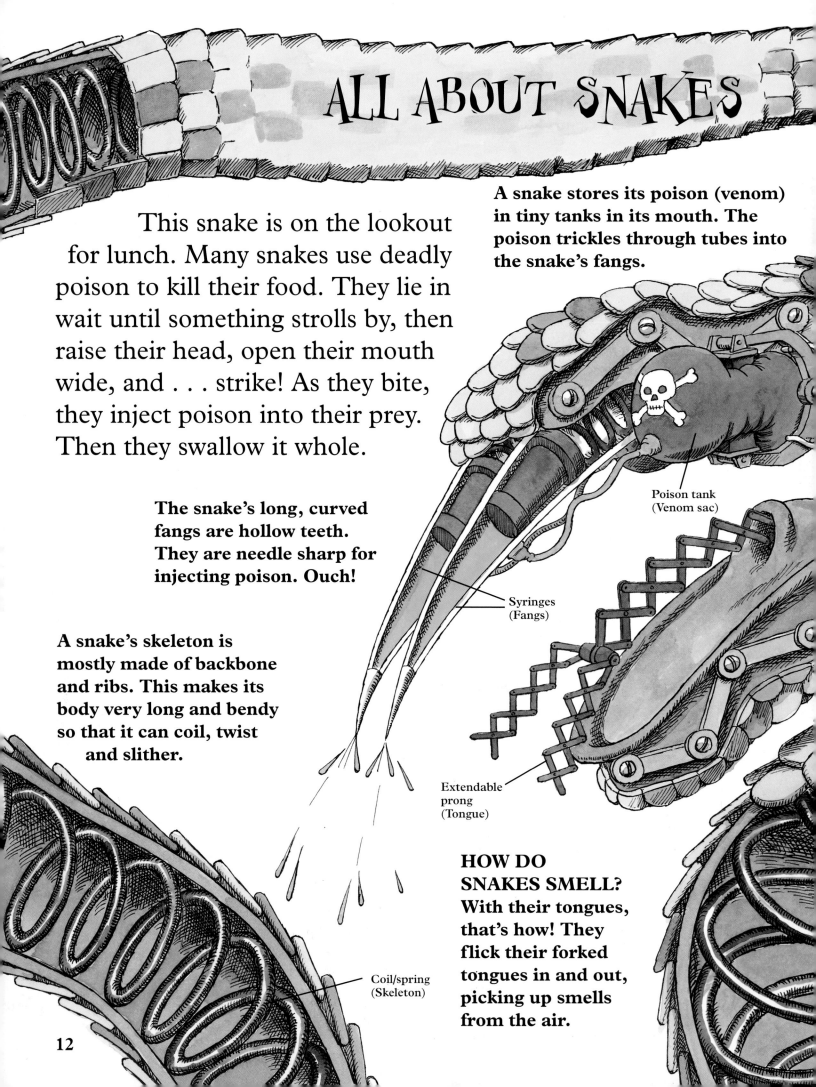

This snake is on the lookout for lunch. Many snakes use deadly poison to kill their food. They lie in wait until something strolls by, then raise their head, open their mouth wide, and . . . strike! As they bite, they inject poison into their prey. Then they swallow it whole.

A snake stores its poison (venom) in tiny tanks in its mouth. The poison trickles through tubes into the snake's fangs.

The snake's long, curved fangs are hollow teeth. They are needle sharp for injecting poison. Ouch!

Poison tank (Venom sac)

A snake's skeleton is mostly made of backbone and ribs. This makes its body very long and bendy so that it can coil, twist and slither.

Syringes (Fangs)

Extendable prong (Tongue)

HOW DO SNAKES SMELL? With their tongues, that's how! They flick their forked tongues in and out, picking up smells from the air.

Coil/spring (Skeleton)

12

Rattle
(Tail)

You'll never outstare a snake! They can't blink because they don't have eyelids. Instead, they have see-through skin to protect their eyes.

Goggles
(Eyes)

To send a warning, a rattlesnake shakes the end of its tail. If this doesn't work, it bites!

A snake can open its mouth very wide to swallow food bigger than its head. This is because it has long, stretchy hinges between its jaws.

Hinges
(Jaw)

Roof tiles
(Scales)

Some snakes wrap their coils around their dinner and squeeze it to death. They are called constrictors.

Venom opening

Venom (poison) sac

Scales

Fang

Rattle
(tail)

Tongue

Jaw

WHAT IS A SNAKE?
A snake is a reptile, an animal with scaly skin, related to lizards and alligators. The reticulated python is the longest snake. It can grow over nine metres long. Tiger snakes are the deadliest snakes.

13

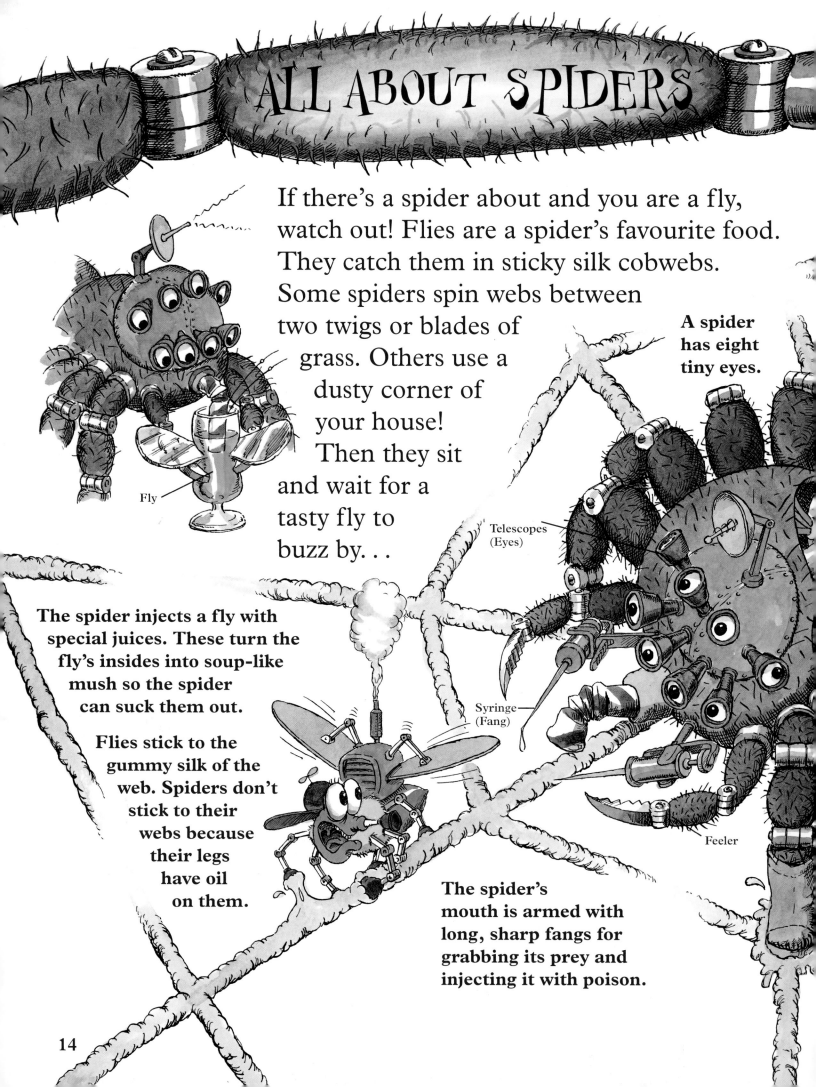

ALL ABOUT SPIDERS

If there's a spider about and you are a fly, watch out! Flies are a spider's favourite food. They catch them in sticky silk cobwebs. Some spiders spin webs between two twigs or blades of grass. Others use a dusty corner of your house! Then they sit and wait for a tasty fly to buzz by. . .

A spider has eight tiny eyes.

Fly

Telescopes (Eyes)

Syringe (Fang)

Feeler

The spider injects a fly with special juices. These turn the fly's insides into soup-like mush so the spider can suck them out.

Flies stick to the gummy silk of the web. Spiders don't stick to their webs because their legs have oil on them.

The spider's mouth is armed with long, sharp fangs for grabbing its prey and injecting it with poison.

14

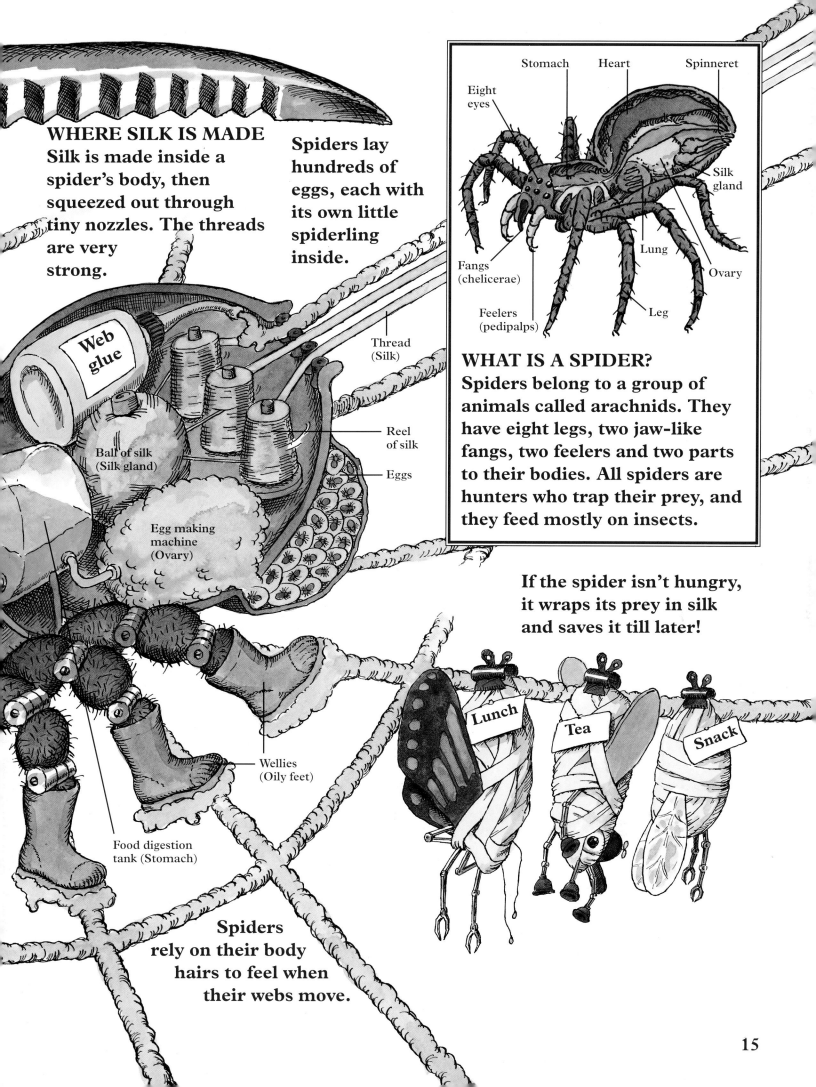

WHERE SILK IS MADE
Silk is made inside a spider's body, then squeezed out through tiny nozzles. The threads are very strong.

Spiders lay hundreds of eggs, each with its own little spiderling inside.

Web glue

Ball of silk (Silk gland)

Egg making machine (Ovary)

Thread (Silk)

Reel of silk

Eggs

Wellies (Oily feet)

Food digestion tank (Stomach)

Spiders rely on their body hairs to feel when their webs move.

Stomach

Heart

Spinneret

Eight eyes

Silk gland

Fangs (chelicerae)

Lung

Ovary

Feelers (pedipalps)

Leg

WHAT IS A SPIDER?
Spiders belong to a group of animals called arachnids. They have eight legs, two jaw-like fangs, two feelers and two parts to their bodies. All spiders are hunters who trap their prey, and they feed mostly on insects.

If the spider isn't hungry, it wraps its prey in silk and saves it till later!

Lunch

Tea

Snack

ALL ABOUT KANGAROOS

Kangaroos are built for bouncing. They bound along the ground on their long, strong back legs, using their tails for balance. Newborn baby kangaroos look nothing like their mothers. They are blind, hairless and only as big as bees. They crawl into their mother's pouch and stay there for the next few months, drinking milk and growing bigger . . . and bouncier!

Kangaroos have large, twitching ears, like radar, for keeping track of what is going on around them.

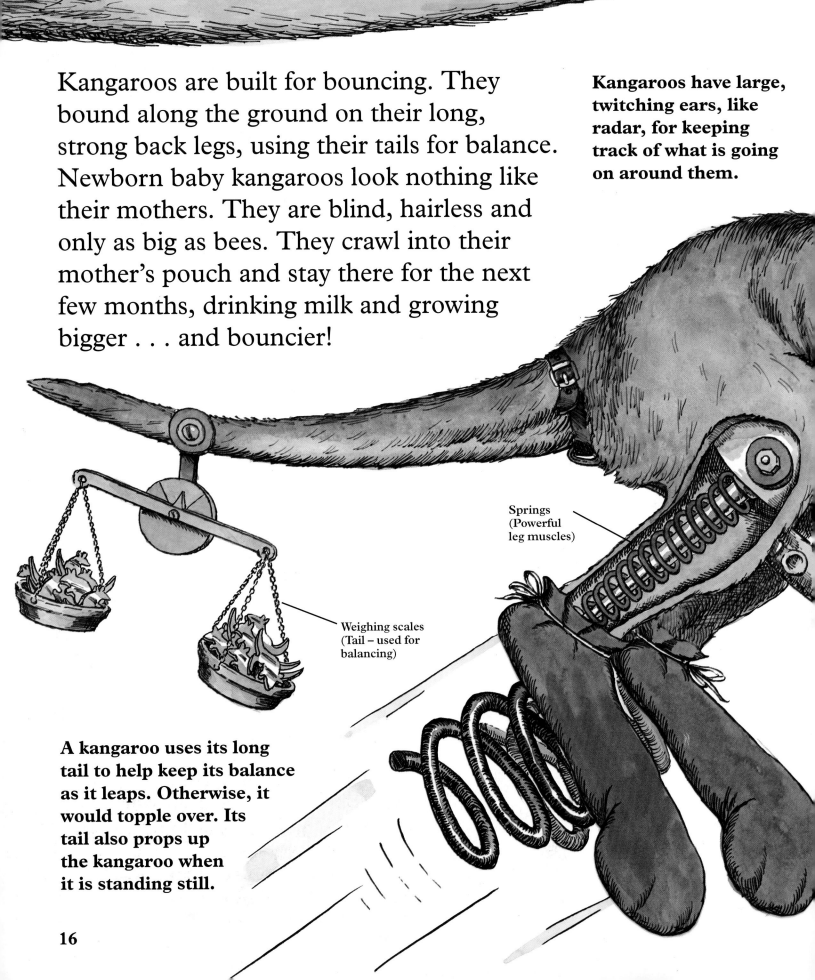

Springs
(Powerful
leg muscles)

Weighing scales
(Tail – used for
balancing)

A kangaroo uses its long tail to help keep its balance as it leaps. Otherwise, it would topple over. Its tail also props up the kangaroo when it is standing still.

In a group of kangaroos the biggest adult male is boss! Rival males fight with their front arms, sharp claws and powerful back legs.

Radar
(Ears)

Boxing gloves
(Powerful front arms)

Joey
(Baby)

Baby carrier
(Pouch)

Baby's bottle
(Teat)

A kangaroo once leapt high enough to clear two cars, one on top of the other. It could have jumped right over you!

There are two types of milk for the joey (baby) to drink. Newborn joeys drink low-fat milk. Joeys that have left the pouch drink a high-fat blend.

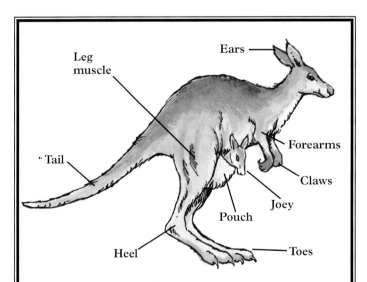

Leg muscle

Ears

Tail

Forearms

Claws

Joey

Pouch

Heel

Toes

WHAT IS A KANGAROO?
A kangaroo is a type of animal called a marsupial. This means it is a mammal with a pouch for holding its baby. Kangaroos live only in Australasia.

ALL ABOUT ELEPHANTS

Everything about elephants is BIG! Their tusks, trunks, ears and appetites! An elephant's trunk is in fact its nose. But it isn't just used for smelling. Elephants use their trunks for drinking, picking up food (and babies!), snorkeling, trumpeting, showering, and spraying on dust and mud to stop sunburn and insect bites.

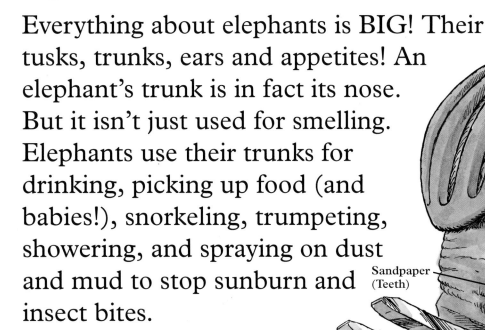

Crash helmet (Strong skull)

Mini flyswatters (Eyelashes)

Fan (Ear)

Sandpaper (Teeth)

Fork (Tusk)

Hose (Trunk)

Elephants use their tusks like forks for digging and lifting.

HOW AN ELEPHANT USES ITS TRUNK

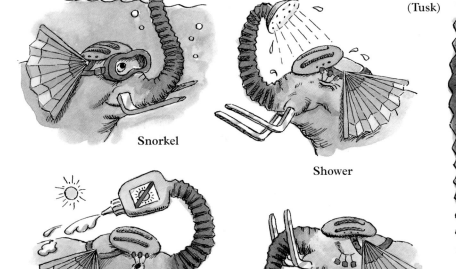

Snorkel

Shower

Sun protection

Smell

DID YOU KNOW. . . ?
Elephants can catch cold, just like you or me. Imagine the size of the hankie you'd need to blow your trunk!

18

African elephants have ears as big as bedsheets. They flap their ears to keep cool.

An elephant breathes through its mouth and trunk. It also uses its trunk like a straw to suck up water.

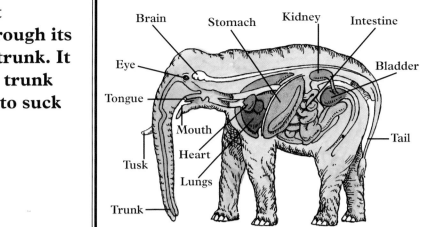

Brain
Stomach
Kidney
Intestine
Eye
Bladder
Tongue
Mouth
Tail
Tusk
Heart
Lungs
Trunk

WHAT IS AN ELEPHANT?
There are two types of elephant – the African and the Asian. The African elephant is the biggest animal on land, and it has bigger ears and more toes on its feet than the Asian elephant.

Bellows (Lungs)

Steel bumper (Rib)

An elephant's ribs are so heavy they don't move when it breathes.

The elephant uses its long eyelashes and hairy tail to swat away irritating flies and ticks. *Whack!*

Flyswatter (Tail)

Pillar (Leg)

Toes

If the juiciest leaves are too high to reach, the elephant simply butts the tree with its head and pushes the whole thing over. Luckily, it has a hard head.

Cushion (Soft sole)

Elephants have huge legs like pillars. Their big, broad feet have soft soles to cushion their weight as they walk.

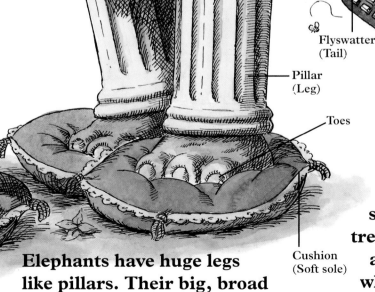

ALL ABOUT OCTOPUSES

There's no mistaking an octopus with its eight rubbery tentacles covered in suckers! Between each "arm" there is a web of skin that helps the octopus swim through the water when it is hunting for crabs, shrimp and fish. The octopus has another trick up its sleeves. It changes colour to show its feelings and to hide from its enemies.

An octopus has big, staring eyes and excellent eyesight for spotting things to eat.

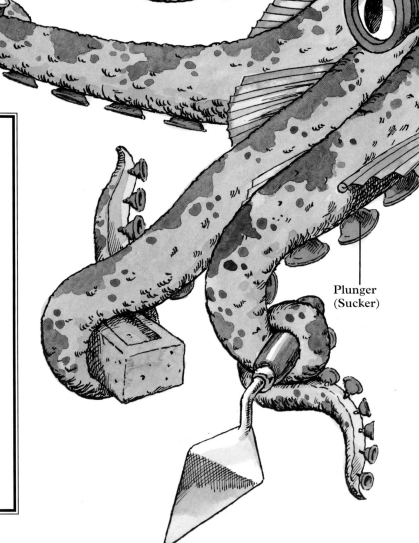

Telescope
(Eye)

Plunger
(Sucker)

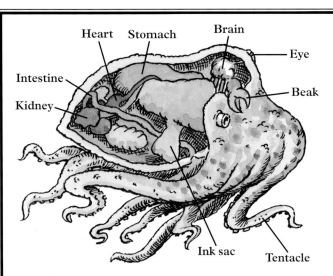

Heart   Stomach   Brain

Eye

Intestine

Beak

Kidney

Ink sac   Tentacle

WHAT IS AN OCTOPUS?
An octopus is a mollusc related to mussels, oysters, snails and squid. Unlike many molluscs, octopuses don't have shells.

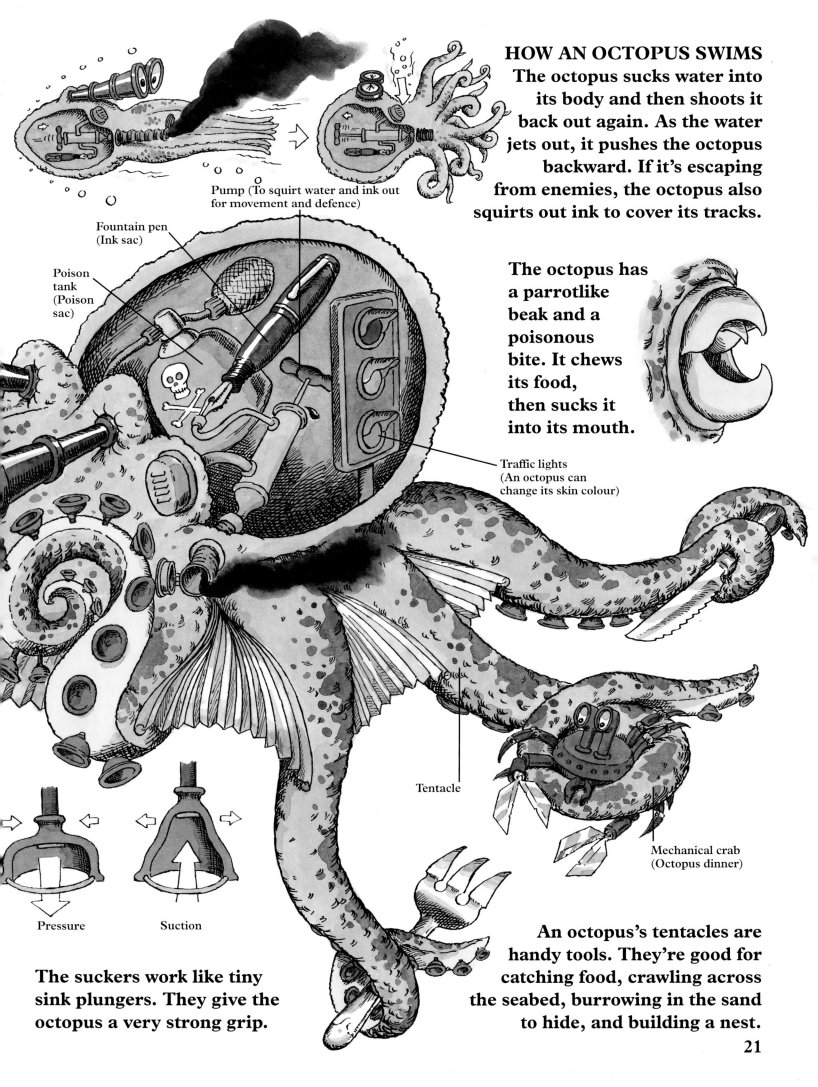

HOW AN OCTOPUS SWIMS

The octopus sucks water into its body and then shoots it back out again. As the water jets out, it pushes the octopus backward. If it's escaping from enemies, the octopus also squirts out ink to cover its tracks.

Pump (To squirt water and ink out for movement and defence)

Fountain pen (Ink sac)

Poison tank (Poison sac)

The octopus has a parrotlike beak and a poisonous bite. It chews its food, then sucks it into its mouth.

Traffic lights (An octopus can change its skin colour)

Tentacle

Mechanical crab (Octopus dinner)

Pressure

Suction

The suckers work like tiny sink plungers. They give the octopus a very strong grip.

An octopus's tentacles are handy tools. They're good for catching food, crawling across the seabed, burrowing in the sand to hide, and building a nest.

ALL ABOUT TORTOISES

With its shiny, armour-plated shell, a tortoise is built like a miniature tank. The shell gives protection to the body, but it is hopeless for hurrying. Tortoises are serious slowcoaches. The great weight of their shells means a tortoise can't move very fast, but it does have extra thick legs to support it.

Tortoises don't have teeth. They grab and cut up food with their sharp, beaklike mouths, then gulp it down. They eat leaves and grass.

The hard bones of a tortoise's skull are like a crash helmet – they protect its head.

Armour plating (Shell)

Crash helmet (Skull)

Grinder (Mouth)

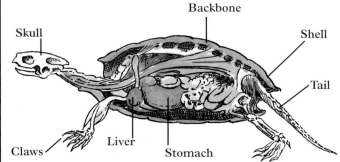

Backbone

Skull

Shell

Tail

Claws

Liver

Stomach

WHAT IS A TORTOISE?
Tortoises are reptiles. The first kind appeared on Earth about 200 million years ago. Tortoises are cold-blooded. They have to live in a warm place for their bodies to work properly.

Retractable hinge (Retractable neck)

A tortoise can pull its head, legs and tail inside its shell for safety.

The tortoise's shell is made of plates of hard bone and horn. These are built up in three layers. The innermost layer is made of the tortoise's backbone and ribs. It forms the framework for the rest of the shell.

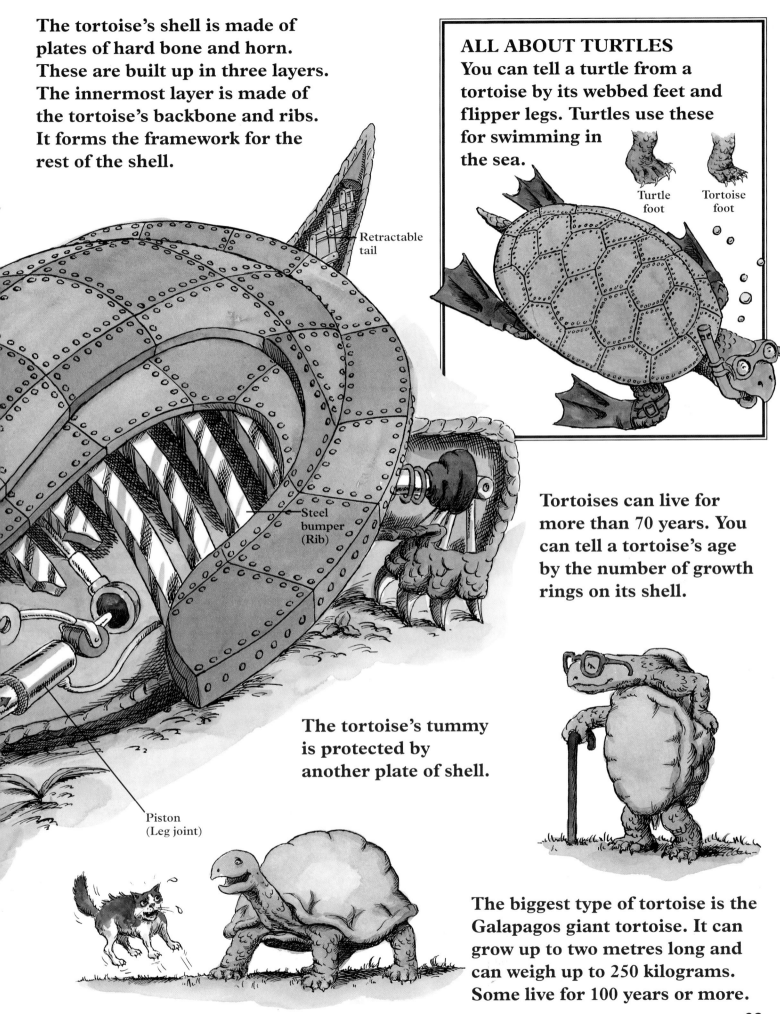

Retractable tail

Steel bumper (Rib)

Piston (Leg joint)

ALL ABOUT TURTLES
You can tell a turtle from a tortoise by its webbed feet and flipper legs. Turtles use these for swimming in the sea.

Turtle foot

Tortoise foot

Tortoises can live for more than 70 years. You can tell a tortoise's age by the number of growth rings on its shell.

The tortoise's tummy is protected by another plate of shell.

The biggest type of tortoise is the Galapagos giant tortoise. It can grow up to two metres long and can weigh up to 250 kilograms. Some live for 100 years or more.

23

ALL ABOUT BATS

The bat's leathery wings stretch between its long, bony fingers and its legs.

Bats are strange-looking creatures with furry bodies and leathery wings. They sleep by day and come out at night to hunt for juicy moths to eat. Bats use sound to find their food. As they fly, they make very high squeaking sounds. The sounds hit an insect and send back an echo. The bat can find the insect from the echo.

Tail

Grabber
(Claw on foot)

Glider
(Wing)

Strut
(Finger
bone)

Hook
(Thumb)

Fruit bats sleep hanging upside down from a branch. They wrap up snugly in their leathery wings. Their back claws lock in place so they don't fall off!

The bat uses its hook-like thumbs for climbing, holding, and combing its fur.

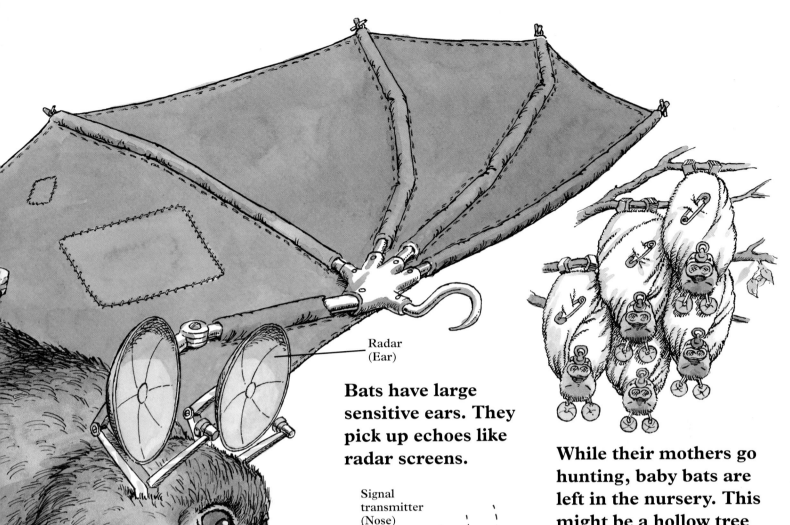

Radar
(Ear)

Bats have large sensitive ears. They pick up echoes like radar screens.

Signal transmitter
(Nose)

Signal transmitter
(Mouth)

Signals

While their mothers go hunting, baby bats are left in the nursery. This might be a hollow tree or a musty cave. Some bat nurseries contain 20 million babies!

Mechanical insect
(Insect dinner)

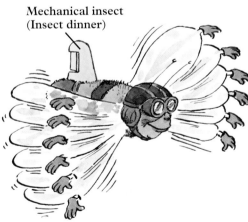

The trick of finding food such as this busy bee is called echolocation. The bat sends out signals from its mouth or nose that hit the insect, telling the bat where to find its dinner!

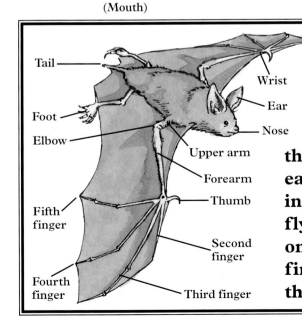

Tail

Foot

Elbow

Fifth finger

Fourth finger

Wrist

Ear

Nose

Upper arm

Forearm

Thumb

Second finger

Third finger

WHAT IS A BAT?
Bats are mammals, like elephants, cows, and you! They are the only mammals that can fly. Some bats eat fruit instead of insects. They are called flying foxes. They rely on sight and smell to find their food, rather than using sound signals.

ALL ABOUT HUMMINGBIRDS

Hummingbirds are tiny, jewel-like birds . . . and amazing acrobats. They can fly forward, backward, up and down. They can even hover in one place, like miniature helicopters. This is useful for drinking the sweet nectar hidden deep inside flowers. But it's hard work staying still. The little bird has to beat its wings so quickly they make a humming noise! *Hmmm. . .*

To hover in one place, the hummingbird has to beat its wings up to 100 times a second. It usually hovers in short bursts with a well-earned rest in between.

Helicopter blades (Wings)

See-saw (Tail)

Hovering uses a lot of energy. The amount of nectar hummingbirds drink in a day to provide this energy is like a person eating 130 loaves of bread!

The hummingbird tips and tilts its tail to keep its balance as it hovers.

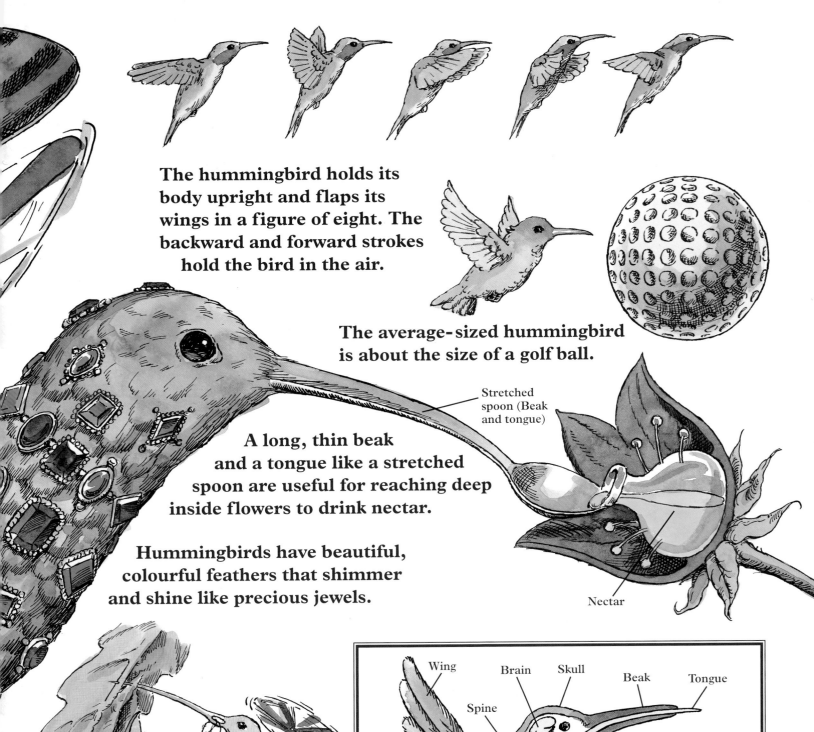

The hummingbird holds its body upright and flaps its wings in a figure of eight. The backward and forward strokes hold the bird in the air.

The average-sized hummingbird is about the size of a golf ball.

A long, thin beak and a tongue like a stretched spoon are useful for reaching deep inside flowers to drink nectar.

Hummingbirds have beautiful, colourful feathers that shimmer and shine like precious jewels.

Stretched spoon (Beak and tongue)

Nectar

Hummingbirds build tiny, delicate cup-shaped nests from feathers, lichen, grass and cobwebs. Some fix their nests with leaves, using spider's silk as glue.

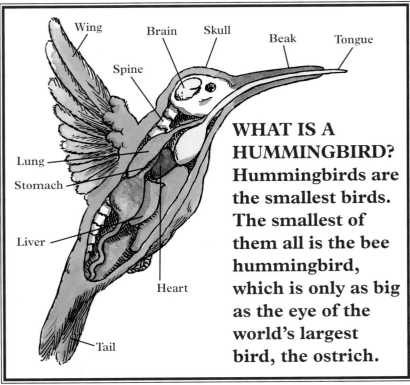

Wing
Brain
Skull
Beak
Tongue
Spine
Lung
Stomach
Liver
Heart
Tail

WHAT IS A HUMMINGBIRD?
Hummingbirds are the smallest birds. The smallest of them all is the bee hummingbird, which is only as big as the eye of the world's largest bird, the ostrich.

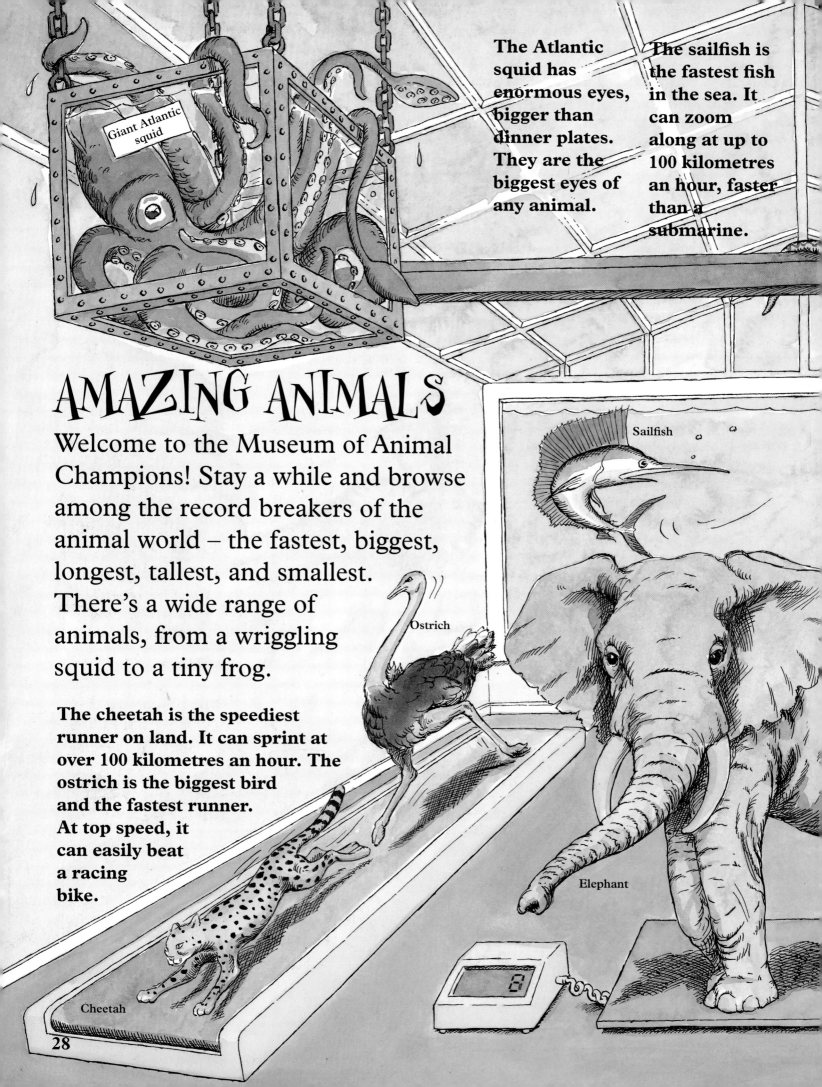

Giant Atlantic squid

The Atlantic squid has enormous eyes, bigger than dinner plates. They are the biggest eyes of any animal.

The sailfish is the fastest fish in the sea. It can zoom along at up to 100 kilometres an hour, faster than a submarine.

AMAZING ANIMALS

Welcome to the Museum of Animal Champions! Stay a while and browse among the record breakers of the animal world – the fastest, biggest, longest, tallest, and smallest. There's a wide range of animals, from a wriggling squid to a tiny frog.

The cheetah is the speediest runner on land. It can sprint at over 100 kilometres an hour. The ostrich is the biggest bird and the fastest runner. At top speed, it can easily beat a racing bike.

Sailfish

Ostrich

Elephant

Cheetah

28

The longest snake is the reticulated python. It is as long as five cars parked in a row.

Reticulated python

Swift

Swift by name, swift by nature! The spine-tailed swift is the fastest bird in the air, speeding along at about 170 kilometres an hour.

Blue whale

Kitti's hog-nose bat

The huge blue whale is the biggest animal ever. Fully grown, it weighs as much as 30 elephants.

Giraffe

Kitti's hog-nose bat is the smallest mammal. This tiny creature is almost three centimetres long, about as big as a large bumblebee.

From its feet to the horns on its head, a male giraffe stands about six metres tall. It's the tallest animal on Earth.

The biggest animal on land is the mighty African elephant. Males weigh about eight tonnes, as much as 60 pigs!

The smallest amphibian is a tiny frog called *Sminthillus limbatus*. It is small enough to fit on your fingernail.

Sminthillus limbatus frog

INDEX